George Washington

A biography of George Washington, one of America's founding fathers

Table of Contents

Introduction 1

Chapter 1: George's Early Years...2

Chapter 2: Pre-Military Career..10

Chapter 3: George's Revolutionary Role 13

Chapter 4: George Becomes President 17

Chapter 5: Retirement 33

Conclusion...37

Introduction

Thank you for taking the time to pick up this book, documenting the life of George Washington.

George Washington lived an incredible life, during a time that can be hard to comprehend. This book details the life of the first President, including his childhood, his time at war, his politics, and his life outside of the public eye.

In the following chapters you will discover the many failures and victories that George Washington experienced in his life. You will learn of his journey to become the first President, and just how impactful he was in the creation and development of the United States of America.

Once again, thanks for choosing this book. I hope that you find it to be insightful and enjoyable!

Chapter 1: George's Early Years

George was born in Westmoreland County, Virginia on the 22nd of February in 1732. Very little is known about when George was a small child and as such, many tales have been passed around, some true and others not. Some of the stories were about when George 'supposedly' after chopping down a cherry tree which his father prized so dearly, threw a silver dollar all the way across the Potomac River. The story has it that he openly confessed to said crime. Did it happen? Probably not. But we will never know for sure.

George was home schooled from age seven to fifteen and studied with their local church sexton. Later on, there was a schoolmaster that taught him in geography, English classics, Latin, and math.

George was lucky to live long enough to be president. He suffered from dysentery, malaria, and pleurisy, all before he was thirty years old. On his way back from one famous expedition, he fell into an icy river off of his raft, and nearly drowned.

When it came to common sense knowledge, the type that would help him survive in life, he learned it through the people he met. Growing up he spent a lot of time around plantation foremen and backwoodsmen. By the time, he was a teenager he already knew how to raise stock, survey land, and grow tobacco.

When George turned eleven, his father died, leaving his half-brother, Lawrence, to finish raising him.

His father's death derailed George's plans to go to England to attend school, as his big brothers had gotten to do. Instead, he would join the Royal Navy. He could enroll as an officer cadet; he would start scraping together the money he needed to buy his commission right away so that when he turned 15 he would be ready.

   Lawrence was good to him, and he had inherited Little Hunting Creek Plantation which was the family's place. He had married well to Anne Fairfax whose father was Colonel William Fairfax.

Anne was good enough to teach George the finer things in life about colonial culture.

When 1748 rolled around, George was sixteen and was traveling with a surveying party and plotting land in and around Virginia's western territory. The next year, with the help of Lord Fairfax, George was appointed to the office of surveyor for Culpeper County. The next two years George was so busy surveying land in Frederick, Culpeper, and Augusta counties that he did not realize how fast time was passing him by. Working like this helped to toughen up his mind and body, and the experience helped make him more resourceful. It also heightened his interest in lands west, and his belief that the future of the United States would lay in going west.

In 1751, Lawrence was very ill with tuberculosis, not a curable disease at that time, but in a last-ditch effort to try to get well, he and George set sail to Barbados. While on their voyage, George contracted smallpox. Smallpox was usually deadly, but George did survive. However, the disease left George's face very scarred. It did make him immune, and this served him well later in the military.

One year later, in 1752, Lawrence passed away of tuberculosis, making George the heir to all the Washington lands. Lawrence's only little girl, Sarah, only two months later, died; and George became the lead of Mount Vernon, one of the most prominent estates in the state of Virginia. George was twenty years old. George was never one to let family tragedy get in the way of work. So, George and three of his best friends from the military talked the governor into splitting his dead brother's job into four different regional jobs and give the posts to the four of them.

He would later convince the Governor's successor that a land grant that was intended to compensate military men was just a bonus for the senior officers. This little scheme, like all others that George hatched up, worked to his advantage and made George a very rich man.

All through his life, he would think that farming was one of the most honorable professions one could have; and he was so very proud of Mount Vernon. He worked and increased the size of Mount Vernon until it was about 8,000 acres.

In some of George's private letters, there is a suggestion that he may have 'carried on,' 'cut a circle,' 'had an affair' with Sally Fairfax, who was married to one of George's closest friends during the Forbes Expedition. Sally and George William Fairfax, her husband, were frequent guests at Mount Vernon until they went back to England where they lived until they died.

He had only left the army about a month however, when George married Martha Dandridge Custis, who was a widow. She was a few months older than George, but that did not matter. Martha was quite rich. To the marriage, she brought 18,000 acres of land. George purchased 6,000 acres of it from her to add to his 8,000 that he already had. Martha brought her two young children. They were ages 4 and 6, and their names were Jacky and Patsy. Washington loved the children as if they were his own and lavished affection on the two of them. He would order them toys from London and managed the Estate to secure their financial future. Martha was not able to have any more children.

As the children grew, Martha made sure Patsy learned feminine skills so she would feel comfortable in Virginia Society. Patsy learned fancy needlework, how to play the harpsichord, and how to perform choreographed dances.

Jacky was to learn the art of being a gentleman. He was taught to speak in public, dance, and to hunt. In 1761, a Scottish Tutor was brought to Mount Vernon to teach Jacky so he would be prepared to go to college.

In 1766 George started switching his crops around from tobacco to wheat. He diversified with his crops, and it helped get him out of debt.

Mount Vernon came to be known for fishing, horse breeding, flour milling, weaving, spinning, and in the 1790's Whiskey production. He hired a trained distiller from Scotland to help with making the whiskey. It wasn't long, and he had built one of the largest distilleries in the United States. When Georges

Distillery was at it's peak, it could put out 11,000 gallons of rye whiskey. This became one of his most successful business ventures.

Around the age of twelve, Patsy started having seizures, which could have been brought on by epilepsy. During those times, it was untreatable. At one point, George, Martha, and Patsy even traveled to Warm Springs, West Virginia so she could partake of the mineral waters that were supposed to have healing properties. There was nothing that stopped Patsy's seizures that only got worse over time. After a violent seizure, June 19, 1773, Patsy died at 17 years old. Martha, per George, was at the lowest ebb of misery. He too was heartbroken when Patsy died.

In 1768 Jacky who never really cared about learning was sent away to boarding school to get him prepared for college. One of his boarding school friends, however, introduced him to one Eleanor Calvert. Their friendship blossomed into a real romance. Before he was to leave to go away to college, they became secretly engaged. George was furious; Martha was happy! George insisted the marriage be postponed, and Jacky went off to college. Martha finally talked George into letting Jacky leave college for good.

On February 3, 1774, just a few months after Patsy had died, Jacky, nineteen and Eleanor, sixteen were married. For eight years, Jacky and Eleanor and their four kids didn't have a home of their own; instead, they divided their time between the Calvert Family home in Maryland and Mount Vernon in Virginia. Martha loved this arrangement. It filled the house with love and laughter of family and children. This happy time did not last very long, however.

November 5, 1781, just a few weeks before he was to turn twenty-seven, Jacky contracted a virulent illness and died. Once again, Martha lost another child. George did not hesitate to adopt two of his children.

The attraction between Martha and George grew over time. It developed into a deep respect, admiration and a mutually abiding affection. Martha was over a foot shorter than George, and when she wanted to get his attention, she would grab his

shirt collar and pull his face down in front of hers. George was
by all accounts a thoughtful and loyal husband. He respected
his wife's opinions and tried to please her in whatever way he
could.

After George retired from the Virginia Military and until the
start of the Revolution, he only worked on caring and developing
his land, managing livestock, rotating crops, and keeping up
with the most current scientific advances. He loved fox hunts,
fishing, cotillions, and horseback riding. He was not a lazy man;
he worked six days a week. More times than not, he would take
off his coat and work right along with his hired hands. He was
an innovative farmer who bred horses, cattle and tended to his
fruit orchards.

He had over 100 slaves, but claimed to never having believed in
slavery. George however did say that he accepted the fact that
slavery was law. He made the decision to get involved in
Virginia politics in 1758.

George Washington's adopted daughter speaks about him and
his relationship with God. She states that while in Philadelphia
or New York he would never omit to go to church in the morning
unless he was sick. Afternoon on Sundays was spent in his
room; while the evening was spent with his family, and not
having any company. Once in a while, an old intimate friend
would drop by for an hour or two; but for the most part, visitors
were prohibited on Sunday afternoons. She said there was no
one that attended church that was more reverent and respectful.
She went on to say that at 9:00 on Sunday evening he would go
into his library where he would stay till 10:00. He was never
one who would act or pray so that others could see him. He was
the kind of man that communed with God in private. His motto
was always, "Deeds, not Words"; and, "For God and my
Country."

According to their church Minister however, Washington was
notorious at their parish church because he refused to kneel
when every one else did during the customary moments in the
Episcopal service. His minister spoke of this disapprovingly
after George died. He said that George was a Deist. Martha was
a devout churchwoman of course, but George never did share

her enthusiasm. Then on communion Sundays, he would always walk out before partaking of the Lord's Supper. He would leave Martha alone to participate.

Because of this one minister, there is a debate about the sincerity of George's Christian beliefs. He was in no way a deist. Deism is defined as a belief that a God created the universe but doesn't himself engage in the lives of women and men. George appealed to "God" and to "Providence" in ways that hinted a divine hand was always there in history propelling America forward.

George was said by his minister never to have taken part in communion. This leads some to doubt that he was a true Christian believer. However, he did serve as a church warden and a vestryman, positions in his church that required he swear that he would not act or speak in any fashion that didn't conform to the doctrines of the church.

The lithurgy of the Falls Church Anglican and their tradition, every Sunday says the Nicene Creed or the Apostle's Creed. These two creeds declare that Jesus is God, that He is the one who died and on the third day rose again, and His death and His resurrection saves all believers.

His personal faith is a matter that is between him and God, but it is more certain than not that he was a deeply religious man.

A common story about George involves his teeth. They caused him suffering his entire life. As early as age 24 he started documenting in journals about his teeth and his problems with them.

He recorded at age 24 that he had to pay five shillings to the dentist who pulled one of his teeth. Other letters and entries in diaries make references regularly to lost teeth, aching teeth, ill-fitting dentures, inflamed gums, and a ton of other dental problems and pain. There is documentation of money paid out to dentists, money spent on teeth scrapers, toothache medication, cleaning solutions, toothbrushes, and denture files, all through his life.

And, the myth about his teeth being made of wood? Nope, not true. They may have been stained up so bad they looked like wood, but they were not. You might be surprised to know that during his life he did use several full and partial denture sets and they were made of different materials like horse teeth, other human teeth, cow teeth, elephant ivory, copper alloy, and possibly brass, silver alloy, and lead-tin alloy.

George knew early on that his teeth were terrible and he was going to run into big trouble eventually. Knowing this, he kept several of his teeth that had already fallen out or been pulled out in a drawer locked up at the Mount Vernon Estate. In a letter on Christmas Day 1782, he wrote to his cousin Lund and asked him to wrap up the teeth and send them to him as he was having some new dentures made. Here is what the letter said:

"In a drawer in the Locker of the Desk which stands in my study you will find two small (fore) teeth: which I beg of you to wrap up carefully, and send enclosed [sic] in your next letter to me. I am positive I left them there, or in the secret drawer in the locker of the same desk."

If you look in some of Washington's accounting books you will find an entry or two that details his purchase of teeth, nine to be exact for 122 shilling from Negroes. It is not known for sure if he ever used the teeth, but it was not unusual in those days for those with money to purchase other human teeth so they could have a set of dentures made.

George had his first full set of dentures by the time he was 57. He owned five sets of dentures. By the time, George was inaugurated the first time; he only had one tooth left. The dentist pulled it and had it put into a little glass display he kept on his watch chain.

Due to the ill-fitting of dentures, artists started noticing significant changes in his face shape. Especially in the shape of his mouth and jaw.

George was very self-conscious about the bad dentures and his appearance. He wrote a letter to his dentist in 1797 that said: "already too wide, and too projecting for the parts they rest upon; which causes both upper, and under the lip to bulge out, as if swelled." Poor George.

Chapter 2: Pre-Military Career

Britain and France in the early 1750's seemed to be at peace. But, the French military kept taking up more and more space in the Ohio Valley. It was said they were there to protect the King's land interests along with the French settlers and fur trappers. The lands bordering this area did not feel good about this move and were prone to dispute the situation. Washington, showing signs of a born natural leader, was appointed Major of the Virginia militia by Robert Dinwiddie, Virginia's Lieutenant Governor.

Not a surprise that a kid whose real life experience so far seemed to consist of sucking up to and schmoozing local socialites, George seemed to do pretty badly as a combat officer.

In 1753, Washington was sent to Fort LeBoeuf in Pennsylvania to tell the French to get out of the land claimed by the Brits. On his way, he made friends with Tanacharison, an Indian Leader who turned out to be very influential and tried to guarantee an alliance with him if war were to break out.

When he got to them, the French declined. Washington made a quick trip back to let them know at the state capitol that the French were not going anywhere. Dinwiddie told George to go back, take some troops and set yourself up at Great Meadows. George did as he was told.

His small group attacked the French post at Fort Duquesne and killed their commander and nine others as well as took the rest as prisoners. Now some researchers feel that it is a bit strange that the commander, Jumonville, was not shot until after he surrendered. No one knows for certain exactly what happened because it was all written by George, so it is felt that it may be written in a self-serving manner. Thus, the Indian and French War had begun. This also came to be known as the Seven Years War.

The French came back at them and drove George and his men all the way back to Great Meadows. After fighting all day,

George surrendered but was soon let go, and he returned to Williamsburg. He promised he would not build another fort on the banks of the Ohio River.

George may not have known how to negotiate a surrender, or how to read French, or knew how to choose high ground for his forts - but he was an expert it seems on being able to shift blame. In his report, he states that he had bad troops and bad provisions as the reason to why he failed the campaign. On top of that, they had to fight in bad weather, and their translator spoke Dutch, not French.

Even with all of that, they gave George the honorary rank of colonel. He soon joined British Braddock's army in 1755 in Virginia. They concocted a three-prong assault on French Forces and attacked Crown Point, Fort Niagara, and Fort Duquesne. In this encounter, the Indian allies of the French and the French themselves ambushed and killed Braddock. George escaped being injured but had two horses shot out from under him and four bullet holes in his coat.

By August of that year, Washington had been promoted to commander of all the Virginia troops, and he was only 23 years old. They sent him to the western frontier with about 700 ill-disciplined troops and a legislature back home that was not willing to support him in any way, while he was supposed to be patrolling and protecting 400 miles of border. His health went downhill, and at the end of 1757, they sent him home with dysentery.

At some point in 1758, George was able to return to duty but on another assignment. He was sent to capture Fort Duquesne. Fire broke out, and 14 of his men were killed along with 26 being injured. They were able to capture the Fort they had gone after and took control of the Ohio Valley. George retired from this regiment in December of 1758.

He felt that his experience during war was simply frustrating, to say the least. Decisions to be made were done excessively slowly, he had no support from his legislature, and all his troops were inadequately trained. George decided to apply for a commission in the British Army, but they turned him down. In

December 1758, he decided to resign his commission and went back to Mount Vernon, his home, a very disillusioned man.

Chapter 3: George's Revolutionary Role

Along came the British Proclamation Act in 1763, which did not allow for settlement beyond the Allegheny Mountains. It irritated George, and he was against the Stamp Act in 1765. George stayed back and kept quiet about his dislikes until the Townshend Acts of 1767. You can tell by his letters from this time that he was totally against the colonies declaring independence. He was not opposed to resisting in what he believed were violations by the Crown of the Englishmen's rights.

In 1769, George introduced what was then called a resolution; but today would be called a bill, for the House of Burgesses; asking that the state of Virginia start boycotting all British goods until they repealed the Acts.

After the Intolerable Acts passed in 1774, George chaired another meeting in which they adopted the Fairfax Resolves. They called for the Continental Congress to convene as a last resort, use armed resistance. George found himself selected as a delegate in March 1775 to the First Continental Congress. George was 43 years old at this time.

After George's battles at Concord and Lexington in the spring of 1775, the political dispute got worse between the Northern colonies and Great Britain, eventually resulting in armed conflict. In May, George attended the Second Continental Congress, and he went dressed in military attire. He wanted them to realize he was ready to fight. June 15th, he became Major General as well as Commander-in-Chief over the colonial forces to go up against Great Britain.

George was the best choice for the job for several reasons: he had the military experience, charisma for the job, he had prestige, and he had been advising Congress for months already. Another factor played into this, and it was political. The Revolution started in the New England area, and at that time only those colonies had been feeling the pinch of the British tyranny. Virginia being the largest British Colony deserved some recognition, and Southern support was what New England would get.

Honestly, George was not skilled in the fighting methods of the British. He was not experienced in the large formations and their massive artillery, but what he lacked in those areas, he made up for in courage and determination. He was smart enough to stay ahead of the British and their game.

Washington with his small army did get a taste of victory in March of 1776. They placed artillery above the city of Boston, forcing the British to have to withdraw. George then moved his men into the city of New York.

In June of that year, a new arrived came on the scene. A new British commander, Sir William Howe. He made it to the colonies with the biggest army Britain had ever deployed to that date.

In August, the British attacked and took back New York in the biggest battle of the entire war. George's army suffered and had to surrender 2,800 of his men. He told the rest of his men to get back across the Delaware River and over into Pennsylvania. General Howe, being ever so confident that the war would be over in just a few months, decided to winter his boys at Princeton and Trenton. This left things wide open for Washington to attack at a place and time he chose.

Martha Washington joined George in the winter every year of the war. They would entertain soldiers and guests. She made it her war too. She would nurse wounded and sick soldiers and raise money needed for the troops. She would take needlework with her to help pass the time during the cold, long winters. When you counted it all up, she would spend about half the war in camp.

Christmas night, 1776, George and his troops crossed over the Delaware River and attacked Howe's troops at Trenton, forcing them to surrender. Within a few days, avoiding an army that had been sent to destroy George and his group, George attacked Howe's boys again and this time at Princeton. This dealt them a humiliating loss.

General Howe, however, wanted to take all colonial cities and stop the rebellion at key political and economic centers. He felt that if American's major cities were withheld from them, their rebellion would be over. During the summer of 1777, he moved against Philadelphia. George moved in to defend the city and was defeated at what was called the Battle of Brandywine. Philadelphia fell about two weeks later.

Late summer 1777, a major force was sent in by the British Army, this time under the command of a man by the name of Burgoyne. He came in south of Quebec into New York to split off the rebellion going on in New England. His strategy backfired. Burgoyne was trapped by American soldiers being led by Benedict Arnold and Horatio Gates, at the Battle of Saratoga. Without the support that he desperately needed, Burgoyne had to surrender his army of 6,200 men. This victory was the major turning point of the war. It is what compelled France to openly ally with the American cause for independence.

During the winter of 1777, George brought in Baron von Steuben to train his men. This Prussian drill sergeant worked with the Continental Army to turn them into some tough fighting machines. When they left Philadelphia, Washington had them fighting at Monmouth. This new army fought the British to a draw. This was considered a major victory for George, and Lee was forced to retire.

George had learned a valuable lesson during all of this: The military nature of war was not the only the important part - the political aspect was important also. He understood that military victories were essential, but not as important as keeping the resistance alive.

George's darkest time in the Army was during the winter at Valley Forge. His 11,000-man army suffered thousands of deaths, with the most of them coming from disease. But, the army came out from that winter intact and in fairly good order.

By the year 1782, the French Army and their navy had left, and the Continental treasury was virtually depleted. Most of George's soldiers had not been paid for several years.

During the war, both the state governments and Congress were extremely short on cash. To make up the difference, and encourage the men to reenlist, they issued vouchers worth up to 600 acres of land to each soldier. The payment of the vouchers was due to the men in the event of victory. But, as always, legislatures were no better with money after than before the war, so the vouchers were being delayed.

George, sensing a possible opportunity, sent one of his brothers out to listen to the men about what they were saying. He wanted to know what they thought of their vouchers. When he found out they were not happy, he bought the men out for pennies on the dollar for their vouchers. By the time he finally died, George owned over 52,000 acres of productive land.

Mutiny was at hand until George convinced Congress to pay the soldiers a five-year grant bonus in March of 1783. By November of that same year, the war was over; the Americans had their independence. George said good-bye to his troops on December 23, 1783, when he resigned as commander-in-chief and went home to Mount Vernon, once again.

For four solid years, George worked hard at resuming life as a farmer and to give his much-neglected plantation the attention and care that it deserved. The war had taken its toll on the Washington family lands, with no exports being allowed and the depreciation of paper money. George was fortunate though in the fact that he was able to repair his land with a generous grant from Congress in return for his military service.

Chapter 4: George Becomes President

In 1787, George was called again for duty to his country. Once
they had achieved independence, they did not know what to do
with themselves and were clashing over the Articles of
Confederation. This was structured so that power was with the
states. But the states could not agree and were not unified.
They were constantly bickering and fighting over land
boundaries, navigation rights, and were refusing to pay off their
part of the nation's war debt.

Washington was still not over the war; but he was keeping his
mouth shut. Once Shay's rebellion broke out however, George
knew then something needed to be done. In 1786, Congress
called a convention that would be held in Philadelphia, where
they desired to modify the Articles of Confederation.

February 4, 1789, 69 men made up the electoral college, and
they voted unanimously that George Washington be the new
country's, first President. The day after the votes were counted,
Charles Thompson, who was the secretary of Congress, went to
Mount Vernon to tell George of the good news.

Now, Thompson was Irish, tall with a narrow face, and his eyes
just penetrated you. There is no way he could have been happy
about making the trip because it was terrible weather. He had
some horrible roads and some large rivers he had to cross just to
get to George. Though it is said that he was so happy that
George was going to be the new president. He felt like God had
sent him to be the "savior or father" so to speak of the country.
George liked Thompson and always thought of him as a faithful
public servant and loyal to his country.

Around noon, April 14th, 1789 George opened the door to his
home in Mount Vernon and greeted Thomson. Once inside the
mansion, each man read from a prepared statement. Thomson
started out by saying he was so honored to have the privilege to
be able to tell George he had been elected unanimously to the
office of President. He then read aloud a letter he had brought

with him from Senator Langdon. Thomson acted as though he was afraid George was going to back out of being President.

Anyone who new Washington would know that he would accept, but with apologies of his inadequacies for the job at hand. George was worried he was not fit for the job as President. It was nothing like he had ever done before. He had high hopes for the new republican government, and he knew that now it all rested in his hands. Before, he had been able to stay out of the public eye and just be a quiet observer, but being president would stop that, and he would have no place to hide. He would now be in public view all of the time!

Whilst he had been waiting to hear the results of the election, it only gave George more time to come up with reasons as to why he should not be president. He was glad he had to wait. He told Henry Knox, his future Secretary of War that it was like thinking about being taken to your place of execution. He loved the "peace" of Mount Vernon, and he didn't feel smart enough to be a president to this new country where there were so many problems to deal with. He felt like the presidency was nothing but a death sentence and when he accepted it that all his privacy and happiness that went along with it would be forever gone.

Washington, knowing what a huge job he had ahead of him, decided he would leave for New York on April 16th. With him would go his aide David Humphreys and of course, Thomson, whose carriage they would take. In his diary he tells about leaving Mount Vernon, his private life, and exchanging it for an oppressed mind and terrible, painful anxiety; more than words could ever express. He went on to say he was answering a call to the service of his country to be obedient, but he did not see that he could ever meet their expectations. He waved good-bye to Martha, who wasn't going to be able to join him until May. Martha watched her husband of thirty years leave, wondering if this had been a good decision and if he would ever be home again. She doubted this wisdom in the act of his public life. She confided in her nephew that she thought it was too late to go into public eye for him. Martha felt their family would never be the same again. Martha was right.

Determined to get to New York quickly, George and his group
got up each day at sunrise and rode a full day. As they rode
along the way, he was hoping to keep distractions to the
minimum, but he was soon to find out that there were to be
eight days of exhausting festivities ahead. He barely got ten
miles north of home when the townspeople there stopped him
and had a dinner in his honor, which went on and on with
thirteen toasts! George was good with goodbyes, and he bade
them a very eloquent farewell.

It did not take long to realize this trip to Washington was going
to be like a Royal Coronation. George was acting like he was
already a politician, making political promises along his trail.
When he went through Wilmington, he spoke to the Society for
Promoting Domestic Manufacturers. In Philadelphia, a group of
local officials met him outside of town and asked him to please
ride a white horse into town they had brought for him. When he
crossed over a bridge on the Schuylkill River, it was decorated
with wreaths, laurels, and evergreens. He was crowned in that
town. Along the way, he heard many times "long live George
Washington." James McHenry, his former aide, told him before
he left home that he was now a king only under a different
name.

When George got to Philadelphia, he was smack dab in the
middle of a full-scale parade. There were 20,000 people that
had come out and lined the streets; all eyes on him. The Federal
Gazette reported that "His Excellency rode in front of the
procession, on horseback, politely bowing to the spectators who
filled the doors and windows by which he passed." George noted
as he moved toward his old haunt, the City Tavern, that church
bells were ringing. The editorial in the newspaper spoke about
how he had united the country. By the next day, George was so
tired of all the partying that when the light horse cavalry came to
ride with him to Trenton, George was already gone. He had left
the city an hour earlier so as to avoid even the appearance of a
parade.

When George came to the bridge over Assunpink Creek near
Trenton, the very spot that he had fought off the Hessians and
British, he noticed the townspeople had erected a beautiful floral

arch in honor of him and wrote upon it, "December 26, 1776" and the proclamation "The Defender of Mothers will also Defend the Daughters." As he got closer, 13 young girls, all dressed in spotless white, came forward with flower-filled baskets and scattered petals around his feet. Sitting on his horse, with tears in his eyes, he bowed a deep bow. He was thinking about the big difference between his former situation as compared to now at this very same spot. Then three rows of women, unmarried ladies, young girls, and married ones – started singing that he had protected fair virgins and matrons alike. All this attention just made George doubt his abilities even more. He worried that the people would expect more of him than he could give.

After all of this, George was hoping beyond hope that he could get into New York without anyone knowing he was there. It was not to be. He had even begged Governor Clinton to 'please spare me any further pomp and circumstance'. Of course, he was fooling only himself if he thought he could slip into the capital without anyone knowing it.

When he reached Elizabethtown, New Jersey, he did behold an impressive sight of five congressmen, three senators, and three state officials waiting for him. He felt a sinking sensation that this welcoming was going to be the grandest one yet; the one to top all the others. Moored to the wharf there was a large barge, freshly painted, all constructed just for him and it had awnings of red curtains at the rear of the barge to keep him from getting wet in case it rained. This barge was to be steered by thirteen oarsmen, all of whom wore white uniforms.

When the barge had drifted out in the Hudson River, George could see the Manhattan shoreline. It was crowded with people, waiting for him and his arrival. A local newspaper said that many ships anchored out in the harbor and were garlanded with banners and flags in celebration of this occasion. When he reached the foot of Wall Street, he was welcome by all sorts of dignitaries. George just wanted things to calm down.

All the streets were packed so tight with people that it took George thirty minutes to get to his new residence at three Cherry Street. The house was in the northeast section of the city, near

the present-day Brooklyn Bridge. Just one week before, the
house's owner, Samuel Osgood, had agreed to let Washington
use it as a temporary residence. Washington's demeanor
changed on his route to his new home. His general mood of high
spirits came over him, especially when he saw the legions of
adoring women. George bowed to the multitudes and even took
off his hat for the ladies at their windows. Many waved their
hankies and threw flowers down in front of him.

The Constitution has nothing to say about an inaugural address.
However, George contemplated a speech for this as early as
January of that year. He asked his friend, David Humphreys, if
he would draft one for him. He had to, as George was so
economical with words, the speech would not have been more
than 25 words long. When Humphreys got done with the
address, it was 73 pages long. Having said that, we do not know
how large his handwriting was, how large the sheets of paper
were and so forth. It is a shame that for posterity, there are only
little snippets of it left here and there.

In this speech, George spent most of his talking time telling
them why he would not be a good president like he was some
criminal. He denied to the crowds that he signed on to the
presidency to enrich himself, even though no one had accused
him of being greedy. But somewhere in his speech, George said
that he had faith in the American People. That we had a plan for
a perfect formulation of popular sovereignty, writing that the
Constitution had brought forth "a government of the people:
that is to say, a government in which all power is derived from,
and at stated periods reverts to, them – and that, in its
operation…is purely a government of laws made and executed
by the fair substitutes of the people alone."

But, this ponderous speech never saw the light of day. George
sent it to James Madison who said it was too long and that its
lengthy legislative proposals could be interpreted as meddling.
So instead, Madison help George write a more compact speech
that would avoid all the problems of the prior speech.

Madison was a whirlwind of energy; he seemed to be everywhere
for George in the early days. He was a huge help to George. He
helped with the inaugural address, wrote the official response by

Congress, then wrote George's response back to Congress, making the circle neat and complete. Madison became a pre-eminent adviser and a confidant to George.

George knew that what ever he did during the swearing-in would establish what would happen for all posterity. He wanted to make sure that whatever they did, it was done to serve as a model precedent. For his part, it was devoutly wished that all the precedents be based on true principles.

George made an important decision, and that was not to wear a uniform for his swearing-in at the inauguration. Instead, he would be up there with patriotic symbols. He would wear a double-breasted brown suit (American Manufacturers), made from broadcloth (woven at the Woolen Manufactory in Hartford, Connecticut). The suit had gilt buttons bearing an eagle insignia on them. To round out this outfit, he would wear white hosiery, silver shoe buckles, and yellow gloves. On inauguration day, George would powder his hair and wear a dress sword on his hip, sheathed in a steel scabbard.

The inauguration was held at a building that had long served as New York's City Hall. It had come to be home for many governments uses. It had hosted the Zenger trial in 1735, the Confederation Congress from 1785-1788, the Stamp Act Congress of 1765, then in 1788 during September it was remodeled into Federal Hall for a suitable home for Congress. There was a covered arcade at the street level and a balcony on the second story. The House of Representatives were situated in a high-ceiling room shaped like an octagon on the ground floor; the Senate would meet in a second-floor room on the Wall Street side. From this one room, George would emerge out onto the Balcony to take the oath of office. It seemed in a lot of ways that the first inauguration was done with a lick and a promise to do better the next time. Everything in the building was done in such a rush as 200 workers were trying to get the building finished before the day of inauguration. Luckily, the final effect was gorgeous. A white building with a blue and white cupola, topped off by a weather vane.

A little after noon on April 30th, 1789, after listening all morning to church bells clanging, many carriages carrying legislators, stopped at George's Cherry Street home. Along with his aide Tobias Lear, and David Humphreys, George stepped into his carriage which led the procession slowly down through Manhattan's narrow streets, stopping 200 yards from the Federal Hall. George getting down from his carriage, walked through the double line of soldiers, walked into the building and up to the Senate Chamber, where all the members of Congress were waiting to see him. When George entered, he made sure to bow to both houses of the legislature. From there he went up front to sit in a very imposing chair. A hush settled over the room. Then Vice President John Adams stood up, and he told George that the time had come. He said that the Senate and the House are ready to attend with you while you take your oath of office as is required by our Constitution. George said he was ready.

They stepped through the doorway and out on to the balcony; a huge roar went up from the gathered crowd. This ceremony being conducted outside would confirm the dedication of the crowds below. George was modest, stately, and deeply affecting. He placed one hand over his heart and then bowed several times to the crowds. A French Minister that was present said that you could see the solemn trust between the George and his people who stood together so packed below him with their faces uplifted to him with such hope in their eyes. Congressman Ames of Massachusetts noted that time had indeed made havoc of Georges' face, and that it already looked 'tired, careworn, and haggard'.

The only constitutional requirement for the president was the swearing in that the President would take the oath of office. The morning of the swearing-in, the Congressional Committee decided to have George place his hand on a Bible. This, of course, led to a frantic, last minute search trying to find a Bible. The Masonic Lodge were the ones to come to the rescue by loaning a thick Bible that was bound in deep brown leather, lying on a velvet cushion. When George appeared out on the portico, the Bible was on a table draped in red.

The crowd grew silent. Robert R. Livingston, Chancellor of New York, gave the oath to George Washington, who was moved visibly. When George finished his oath, he bent forward, seized the Bible and brought it to his lips. You could tell that at this moment, George felt this from the very bottom of his soul. One observer also noted the "devout fervency" that he repeated his oath and the reverential manner in which he bowed to kiss the Bible." Now, some say that he added himself at the end, "So help me God," though this was never reported until 65 years later.

Livingston then lifted his voice and as loudly as he could say, "It is done." "Long live George Washington, President of the United States."

Once the balcony ceremony was finished, George went back inside to the Senate Chamber so he could deliver the inaugural address. Congress rose when he entered the room, and once George bowed they all sat down.

When George started his first speech, he seemed nervous, flustered and shoved his left hand into his pocket as he turned his pages with his trembling right hand. His voice was so weak it could barely be heard in the room.

In the first line of his address, George spoke of his anxiety about him being fit for the job of President and told those in attendance that there had never been an event that had ever filled him with such a sense of anxiety before, than the news that was delivered to him by Charles Thomson. He acknowledged that he had grown despondent when he considered his lack of practice when it came to civil government. He told them that the only thing that brought him any comfort was that God had overseen the birth of America. He went on to say that National policy should be rooted in private morality and this relied on the eternal rules of right and order, and that was sanctioned by heaven itself.

After his speech, George led a large procession up Broadway to an Episcopal prayer service at St. Paul's Chapel; He was given his own pew that was canopied. When devotions were over, George finally had a chance to relax before the evening's festivities began.

That night, Lower Manhattan was nothing but a shimmering fairyland of lights. There were two hours of fireworks.

At the meeting, George was voted unanimously picked as the president. Others, such as Alexander Hamilton and James Madison along with George realized that it was not amendments that needed to be added or changed, but a completely new constitution that would give the national government more authority.

Before the convention ended, they produced the plan for government that would not just take care of their current issues but would endure for generations to come. When the convention was over, George's reputation and his support for the new government were essential to the constitution. There were, of course, those who opposed some aspects of the constitution. People like Sam Adams and Patrick Henry condemned the entire constitution as a grab for power.

After the U.S. Capital had been moved from New York to Philadelphia, George hated the food that was being cooked. He brought his own black slave Hercules from Mount Vernon to prepare his meals for him. Pennsylvania had a law in place that stated that slaves who had lived there for six months, would be given their freedom. So, to avoid this happening, just before the six months were up, George would send Hercules back to Mount Vernon. He would wait several weeks and bring Hercules back to the Capital. Hercules was smart, so one night, before George's term was about up, Hercules disappeared and was never heard from again.

After his first term, all George wanted to do was to go back to his beloved Mount Vernon and retire. But, once again was called to serve his country! There was a presidential election in 1789, and he got a vote from every elector from the electoral college. George took his oath of office at the Federal Hall in the Capital of the United States at that time, New York City.

George knew that as the first president, he would be setting a precedent for all future presidents. He was very careful in the way he carried out his duties and responsibilities. He was ever vigilante to not bear any resemblance of any European Royal

Court. So, to avoid that, he preferred the title, "Mr. President."
At first, he did not want to be paid as he had enough money.
Congress finally talked him into being paid for his work to avoid
the impression that only men of wealth could serve as the
president.

George made a deal with them. He asked instead that he would
be paid for his expenses as commander-in-chief during the war.
If he had accepted the initially proposed salary, it would have
been $500 a month and came to a total of $48,000. But with
the deal he made, his expense account came to $447,220, at its
smallest estimate!

George proved to be a great President. He surrounded himself
with some very capable men.

- Thomas Jefferson – Secretary of State

- Alexander Hamilton – Secretary of the Treasury

- Henry Knox – Secretary of War

- Edmund Randolph – Attorney General

The constitution does call for the creation of executive
departments; but it only defined that these heads were to be
unelected officials and were to answer directly to the president.
Our current cabinet includes sixteen members counting the
vice-president.

George soon found out that variance ensured differing ideas
were presented, but it also created tension, and when it came to
debates regarding the establishment of a national bank, well it
almost broke out in fights. Even with all the disagreements,
Jefferson felt that it had no impact on the quality of the way they
governed.

He was thoughtful as he delegated authority and consulted with
his cabinet before he made decisions. He established a broad
range of presidential authority, but he always did so with high
integrity while being honest and exercising power, and restraint.

By doing this, he set a high standard, which has rarely been met by his successors.

During his first term in office, George signed into law measures to reduce the debt of the nation and place its finances back on sound ground. He established several peace treaties with Native Indians, and approved a bill maintaining that the nation's capital would have a permanent district along the Potomac River. Then, he signed the bill authorizing a tax on distilled spirits.

May 31, 1790, George signed into law that is still very important today, and that was the first Copyright Act of 1790. It was an act to encourage learning by securing copies of charts, books, and maps for the proprietors and authors of them during the times stated herein.

Washington's schedule was set so that he could get business done without being interrupted. In the late afternoon, he would meet with the public; evenings would be for invited guests for dinner parties. Tuesday afternoons he would meet with male visitors from three to four p.m. Then, a less formal affair was held on Friday evenings that included both men and women, which fostered interaction with other politicians and colleagues.

Since the settlement of the colonies in North America, Days of Thanksgiving had been celebrated every year. In 1789, George decided to make it a formal holiday. He issued a proclamation that said November 26th would be a national holiday of Thanksgiving. The proclamation was sent to all the state governors, letting them know they were expected to observe this holiday in each of their states. George celebrated the day by going to church at St. Paul's Chapel located in New York City and donated food and beer to imprisoned debtors.

When it came to foreign affairs, George was cautious. He knew that being a young but weak nation, he had to be careful not to give in to Europe's political scams. In 1793, Great Britain and France were at it again. Alexander Hamilton urged George to ignore the mess, and he did.

While serving as President, George only vetoed only two bills. The first was a bill that aimed at providing some guidelines for the how many representatives you should have in Congress based on the 1790 census.

In 1797 on February 28th, George vetoed a bill that aimed at cutting the cost and the size of the military.

When George gave his second inaugural address, it was the shortest that has ever been delivered. It was held on March 4, 1793. It was less than two minutes and had only 135 words. It bears repeating:

 "I am again called upon by the voice of my country to execute the functions of its Chief Magistrate. When the occasion proper for it shall arrive, I shall endeavor to express the high sense I entertain of this distinguished honor, and of the confidence which has been reposed in me by the people of United America." "Previous to the execution of any official act of the President the Constitution requires an oath of office. This oath I am about to take, and in your presence: That if I am found during my administration of the Government I have in any instance violated willingly or knowingly the injunctions thereof, I may (besides incurring constitutional punishment) be subject to the upbraiding of all who are now witnesses of the present solemn ceremony."

George Washington's farewell address when he left office was so profound that in the middle of the Civil War, on February 19, 1862, President Lincoln declared that Washington's Birthday be a national holiday.

Since 1986, on his birthday, all 7,641 words of his farewell address are read by a sitting Senator. At the end of the reading, that chosen Senator writes his thoughts on what the significance of that address means down in the pages of a leather-bound book that is kept by the Secretary of State. The Senator who has written his thoughts then signs with his signature.

In 1794, George sent John Jay over to Britain to try and negotiate the 'Jay Treaty" to secure peace with Britain and clear up some of the left-over issues from the Revolutionary War.

This caused Thomas Jefferson to blow up! He supported the French and he thought the U.S. should honor its obligations of the treaty. George was able to gain public support for the treaty, which eventually proved resolute in gaining ratification in the Senate. It was controversial alright, but the treaty did prove to be beneficial to the United States. It removed British forts from the western frontier, established clear boundaries between the United States and Canada, and the most important part; delayed war with Britain and provided more than a decade of trade that was prosperous and developmental, just what a fledgling new country needed desperately.

During his two terms as President, George was very dismayed at the division he saw among the government and the nation. The power was bestowed on the Federal government, and then the people joined together to influence their decisions (just like today). The formation of different political parties at first were more influenced by personality than by issues.

As Secretary of the Treasury, Alexander Hamilton steamed ahead for a strong national government with the economy built upon industry. Hamilton's version took on the name of Federalist. Secretary of State Thomas Jefferson however, felt the government should be kept small and center the power down to the local level. Jefferson's followers took on the name of Democratic-Republicans. This would let citizen's have their freedom more protected. He felt the economy should be based on farming. Washington himself hated political bipartisanship. He believed that belief differences should never become established as such. He felt strongly that political leaders should have the ability to debate openly and freely without being bound by party lines.

George could do little to impede the progression of political parties. The ideas promoted by Jefferson and Hamilton brought forth a two-party system that proved to remain durable over time.

George had his critics, and in this day and time, he would probably have the same criticisms made. Most critics questioned his spending. George rented the most expensive houses available, was driven in a coach pulled by four horses, and was served by lackeys and outriders wearing rich uniforms. Being overwhelmed by people coming by, he finally announced that with exception of his weekly scheduled reception which was open to all, he would only be seeing people by appointment. George entertained extravagantly, but he did this only in private dinners and only by invitation. Some accused him of acting like a King.

While serving as president; in Europe, a major war started. George, knowing how weak his new nation was, declared the United States as neutral. A French ambassador showed up on the horizon, Citizen Genet, who came to America to set up democratic societies inside the city. George did not trust French illuminism and the way it reigned by terror. He expelled the Citizen Genet from the United States.

Thomas Jefferson was furious and resigned as Secretary of State. George was proven right on his stance when Napoleon began rising to power.

Let's take a look at a few more laws that George Washington enacted as President:

• The Judiciary Act of 1789 – this established the position of Attorney General and a six-member Supreme Court.

George's first group was two justices and ten court judges for the districts. They were to begin service two days after the act was passed. His last appointed judge was just twelve days before the end of his presidency.

Since he was the first President, it made him responsible for appointing an entire Court; he appointed ten justices, two Chief Justices one former Justice. He nominated Robert Harrison who turned down the appointment and William Cushing who also declined.

George appointed 28 judges to the district courts because of the small size at the time of the judiciary; there were fewer states, and most states had only one district court and each of those only needed one judge. Since intermediate appellate courts on the federal level hadn't been created, George had all he needed with the 28. Richard Peters Jr. served the longest of all his appointments, and he served for 36 years.

They decided that the first meeting would be in New York City on February 1, 1790, but only three of the six showed up. It was delayed until the next day. By guidance of the Judiciary Act, they had Chief Justice John Jay, and five Associate Justices: Blair, Cushing, Wilson, Iredell, and Rutledge.

These men met twice a year. One session would be held the first Monday in February and the second session would be held on the first Monday in August.

These men were required to "ride" or travel if you will by horse or buggy. The circuit courts met twice a year, and each justice was given three circuits geographically. Each one spent many months out on the road and logged thousands of miles.

• Naturalization Act of 1790 – formulated rules necessary to be followed to become a United States citizen.

• Residence Act of 1790 – Directed that Washington D.C. be the permanent federal capital, sitting along the Potomac River.

• Coinage Act of 1792 – Developed the U.S. Dollar as our official currency and the United States Mint.

• Militia Acts of 1792 – The two acts that would allow a President to order out the military when threatened by domestic or foreign threats, which created a more structured and regulated military.

• Fugitive Slave Act of 1793 – It became a federal crime to help slaves escape and developed a system that would get escaped slaves back to their rightful masters.

• Naval Act of 1794 – Ordered the building of six warships and created the U.S. Navy.

• Pinckney's Treaty (1795) – Treaty with Spain of friendship to clarify borders between Spanish and US held territories. This opened up the Mississippi River for American Commerce.

• Treaty of Tripoli 1796 – An agreement to pay the Pasha of Tripoli a yearly tribute for its use and unmolested access to the Mediterranean shipping lanes.

And while he was President we gained five more states:

1.   North Carolina – 1789

2.   Rhode Island – 1790

3.   Vermont – 1791

4.   Kentucky – 1792

5.   Tennessee - 1796

Chapter 5: Retirement

George did not want to run a third term; he was feeling the decline of his physical body as he had aged and it was his desire to go home to Mount Vernon. In being the 'first President," he wanted to make sure that there was a peaceful transition to the next President.

During his last few months as President, George felt he must give his country one last message. With the assistance of Alexander Hamilton, he wrote his Farewell Address to the people. He urged the citizens to cherish their union, and to avoid permanent foreign alliances and partisanship. In March 1797, he turned the presidency over to John Adams. He then returned to his beloved Mount Vernon, determined to live out his years as a simple farmer.

George, felt he had left the Government in very capable hands. The country was at peace, debts were resolved and being well-managed, and it was set on a course for prosperity. George was perceived to be wealthy, but his land was only slightly profitable.

While he had been gone for the past eight years, his plantation had suffered, and there was so much work to be done. It was a cold day in December of 1799; George had spent much of the day out on the farm in a terrible snowstorm. When he got home, he ate his supper very fast in his wet clothes and went to bed. He complained about a cough, and being hoarse and he had a runny nose. The next morning, he awoke with a terrible sore throat and became increasingly hoarse. He went to bed early, but woke back up around 2:00 a.m. clutching his chest, having difficulty breathing, and told Martha that he felt sick. Martha wanted to get help, but George was worried about her getting sick since she had just gotten over a cold too. Martha asked Col. Tobias Lear to please come to George's room. When Tobias entered the room, he immediately could see how ill George was, and he sent for Dr. Craik. He had been the doctor for George for over forty years. He also sent for the estate's overseer, Rawlins, who knew all about bloodletting.

By 6:00 a.m. George had a high fever. His throat was painful, and he was having trouble breathing.

At 7:30 a.m., Rawlins removed 12-14 ounces of Georges blood. George asked that they remove some more. Then they gave him some vinegar, molasses, and butter. This almost choked poor George to death because his throat was so swollen and infected.

At 9:00 a.m., Dr. Craik applied a painful "blister of cantharides," also known as "Spanish fly," and placed around George's throat. Supposedly, the blisters this would raise would pull out the toxic stuff causing the inflammation.

At 9:30 a.m., more bloodletting of 18 ounces was performed and another similar one again at 11:00 a.m.

At 12:00 noon, George was given an enema.

They had him attempt to gargle with a tea of sage and vinegar, but this was unsuccessful. George was still able to walk around the room some and then sit up in a chair for a few hours. Once he laid back down however, it was again hard for him to breathe.

Dr. Craik again ordered more bleeding! This time, they pulled 32 ounces. This was getting ridiculous in modern medicine's eyes.

At 4:00 p.m., Dr. Brown arrived. He thought a dose of calomel and tartar emetic, guaranteed to make George vomit with a vengeance.

After the last 32 ounces had been bled out, George appeared to rally a little.

At 5:00 p.m., he seemed to be swallowing easier. He even had enough energy to examine his will with Martha. In his will George made a step considered bold by some and that was to free all his slaves upon Martha's death. His will also stipulated that the older slaves that were too old to work or ones that were too sick to work, be supported by funds from his estate. This worried Martha, in her thinking they may kill her in order to be free upon her death, so she let them all go free on January 1,

1801. He was the only Founding Father that owned slaves ever to do so.

George told the doctors that he died hard and was not afraid to go. That from the beginning he did not think he would survive this and he just didn't think he could last much longer.

George thanked all three doctors for working so hard.

At 8:00 p.m., they placed blister of cantharides on his arms, legs, and feet and wheat poultices on his throat.

At 10:00 p.m., George murmured a few words about burial. He settled back in his bed; took his pulse calmly, then his fingers dropped off of his wrist, and he drew his last breath. The First President of our great country was gone. At his bedside were his wife, Martha, Tobias Lear, his valet, James Craik, his doctor, Christopher Sheels, and three housemaids.

There was arguing among the doctors as to the exact cause of death, but they finally agreed upon inflammation and swelling of his glottis, upper trachea, and larynx that was severe enough to obstruct his airway.

In the year of 1799, George's doctors felt they were justified in removing over 80 ounces of his blood. This was about 40 percent of what his total volume of blood would be. They felt this would reduce the inflammation in his 'windpipe' and help constrict blood vessels in that area. When in fact, this amount of blood loss, with dehydration, viscous blood flow, and electrolyte imbalance could not help, but more than likely hastened the President's death.

After George had died, another doctor arrived. He was an expert in tracheotomy procedures, which in that day was extremely rare and only performed in dire emergencies. But, being that he was too late to perform, it will never be known if it would have made a difference.

In the time lapse of 215 years since poor George died, there have been many guesses as to his terrible demise. Here are just a few: quinsy, Vincent's angina, streptococcal throat infection, diphtheria, acute pneumonia, Ludwig's angina, and croup. The idea of Acute Bacterial Epiglottitis seems more likely than anything else, however, we will never know for sure.

News about his death spread rapidly, plunging the new nation into deep mourning. Cities and towns held mock funerals, and many presented eulogies in honor of their fallen hero. When news of his passing reached Europe, the British fleet paid their tribute to George's memory, and even Napoleon ordered mourning for ten days.

Conclusion

Thank you once again for choosing this book.

I hope that you enjoyed learning about George Washington, and the incredible life that he lived.

If you enjoyed this book, please take a look at my other titles available on Amazon, and don't forget to leave a review!